Bread is a Simple Food
Teaching Children about Cultures

by

Cherry Steinwender

Illustrated by Lowell Hildebrandt

AuthorHouse™
1663 Liberty Drive
Bloomington, IN 47403
www.authorhouse.com
Phone: 1-800-839-8640

First published by AuthorHouse 2/21/2011

ISBN: 978-1-4520-8561-6 (sc)

Library of Congress Control Number: 2010915274

Printed in the United States of America

Any people depicted in stock imagery provided by Thinkstock are models,
and such images are being used for illustrative purposes only.
Certain stock imagery © Thinkstock.

This book is printed on acid-free paper.

authorHOUSE®

Author's Note

BREAD CAN TEACH A POWERFUL LESSON

Bread comes in different sizes, shapes, colors, and textures. Even so, it's all bread. Little children also come in different sizes, shapes, and colors, but they all belong to the same human race.

Bread is such a simple food, right? That is what many school children think before experiencing the innovative workshop entitled, "Opening the Breadbasket." Through this basic food, children can learn a profound lesson about cultures.

Opening the Breadbasket is a 30-45 minute interactive workshop designed and facilitated by the Center for the Healing of Racism for elementary schools. The workshop is designed to help students understand more about and develop an appreciation for differences. By sampling an assortment of breads from around the world, children have the opportunity to learn about the different histories, meanings, shapes and tastes of breads eaten throughout the world. The lesson helps them understand and appreciate different cultural perspectives, beliefs and practices.

As they sample breads from different parts of the world, young children use all of their senses and have a bit of fun as well.

This book was written to help children internalize the oneness of the human family.

I would like to thank Barbara Abell, Marilyn Douglas-Jones, Sylvia Mayer, Melanie Mouzoon, Samantha Stark, and Emma Williams for making this book possible.

Cherry Steinwender

"Good morning!" Ms. Cherry greeted her class as they settled into their chairs. "As we near the last day of school, I would like for us to have a very special Show-and-Tell Day that will bind us together and give us something very special to remember each other by in the coming years."

"We have classmates whose families moved to the USA after their birth; some are the first generation, and others are second or third generation Americans. We even have classmates whose ancestors have always lived here. What I would like this Show-and-Tell to focus on is the bread that your family would eat in their country of origin. Some of you may still eat the bread of your family's homeland, since people rarely leave their cultures behind when they cross borders to make new homes. Some of you may have to ask your parents or grandparents to help you find or make the bread of their native land."

"Think how wonderful it would be to see bread in different colors, sizes and shapes. What is even more exciting is to think that, like bread, all girls and boys come in different colors, sizes and shapes."

On the morning of Show-and-Tell Day, the children arrived very early with lunch boxes and large bags, eager to share the breads of their cultures. Because everyone wanted to be first, many hands were waving in the air. It was difficult for the teacher to decide who should be first. Finally, she chose Gennet, whose family came from **Eritrea and Ethiopia**.

Gennet opened a big and heavy bag. She pulled out a very large grey-colored bread called **Injera** (n-JER-ah). Her classmates looked on with awe, for they had never seen bread so big or so grey. As she passed pieces around, they discovered it felt like a wet sponge.

Gennet told her friends that the way her family eats **Injera** is to take one out of the pack and place it on a plate. Next, they put the meat and veggies on top and eat it all with their fingers.

That was not all. Gennet shared another kind of bread her family enjoys. This one was big and round with different symbols carved into the top. "It's called **Ambasha** (am-BAH-sha) and can be eaten like most bread by breaking off small pieces," she explained.

Tommy could hardly wait his turn. The moment Gennet finished sharing the **Ambasha**, he waved his hand wildly, "Choose me, please, choose me next!" When the teacher signaled his turn, Tommy rushed to the front of the class and took from his lunch box a tiny, tiny, tiny bread that was very dark in color. "My mother calls this a '**Party Rye**,'" he said. Rye is grown primarily in Eastern, Central and Northern **Europe**. The main rye belt stretches from northern **Germany** through **Poland**, **Ukraine**, **Belarus**, **Lithuania** and **Latvia** into central and northern **Russia**. Rye is also grown in **North America** (**Canada** and the **USA**) and in **South America**.

The bread was so small the children giggled as they tried to guess how many sandwiches they would have to eat to consider it a meal. Tommy explained that **Rye Bread** comes in many sizes and shapes, but **Party Rye** is easier to share.

Next, the teacher chose Faizi and Bahji, twins who were holding a large box between them. Their classmates could not take their eyes off the box, wondering what size bread could possibly be in it.

Faizi explained that in his home they eat many different types of breads from the Middle East, and he was proud to show the class more.

Bahji reached into the box and pulled out a large flat round bread she called **Noon**. "**Noon O Pander** is what we usually eat for breakfast or with cheese for snacks. It's easy to carry and keep because it's flat. The pocket can be stuffed to make a sandwich, or it can be eaten with stew or dips. Americans call it **Pocket Bread,** or **Pita** (PEE-tuh)."

Faizi knew the next bread would really wow the children. **Barbari** (bar-bar-ree) is a very long, flat bread with sesame seeds on top. It could easily feed the entire class. But he did not stop there. Next, he showed off **Lavash** (LAH-voish), a very thin bread that was bigger than a desktop when unfolded.

Bahji finished by showing **Iranian Sweet Bread** with raisins.

Zoe and Zach had their classmates on the edge of their seats as they told them about the customs surrounding their family's traditional breads. "**Challah** (HAH-lah) is a very beautiful and delicious bread," said Zoe, "that's braided three times before baking. It's eaten on the Sabbath to remind Jews of their relationship to God and the land of Israel." Zach and Zoe told their classmates how they loved the Passover because of the special meal called a "Seder," where everyone eats **Matzo** (MAT-suh), a flat, hard bread that doesn't rise when baked. Zoe and Zach told them that Jews eat **Matzo** for eight days during Passover to remember that they were once slaves in Egypt. "Now that we are free," the twins told them, "we have a duty to help others become free."

Zoe and Zach's classmates learned a lot about bread and about the history of the Jewish people.

Chirag smiled gently as he neared the front of the class. He and his family came here from India when he was a small boy, and many of the foods and breads eaten in his home are from India.

Chirag held up a bread he called **Naan** (NAWN). "Some **Naan**," he said, "is called **Tandoori Naan** (tahn-DOOR-ee NAWN) after the large stone ovens the **Naan** is baked in." The children loved the soft chewy texture of the bread. "We also make crispy flat breads that are spicy and crunchy, like chips." He showed them a bright orange round bread. "This one is called **Chapati** (che-pah-TEE)."

Maria, whose parents are from Mexico, could not ignore the smell of the **Tortillas** (tore-TEE-Yuhs) her father had made earlier that day for her to share with her friends. She had been nibbling on the bread before the class began.

Fortunately, there were enough **Tortillas** and **Bolillos** (bow-LEE-Yohs) left for her to share. The **Tortillas** were round and very thin, and she had both corn and flour **Tortillas** to share. "The flour **Tortillas** are called **Gorditas** (gore-DEE-tahs) when served with butter and sugar," she told them. "The **Bolillo** is a sweet white bread shaped like a small football. It's delicious when toasted for breakfast or sandwiches."

Siegfried wanted the children to know that he was born in Austria, but his family members are in Germany and Switzerland, so his family eats many types of breads. He brought **Pumpernickel**, (PUMP-er-nickel), a German **Black Bread**, and **Kaiser Rolls. Kaiser** (KI-zer) is a German word meaning king. In Germany the king was such an important person that a roll was named in his honor.

The students thought it was funny to name a bread after a king. Siegfried told them that in the USA we can buy bread called **Hawaiian King Bread** – also named after a king. **Hawaiian King Bread** is a unique Portuguese sweet bread that was first baked in Hawaii.

Yvette jumped from her chair in glee when her name was called. The slightly mischievous smile on her face alerted the teacher that she was up to something! She pulled out her bread –a **Croissant** (krwuh-SAWN) – and asked all of the adults in the room to close their ears. She whispered to her classmates, "The answer to the question I will ask the adults is Vienna, Austria, as told by many Austrians."

Yvette knew that many people are not aware that the **Croissant** was first made by bakers to honor the sounding of the alarm, which led to the defeat of the Turks, at a time when Turkey and Austria were at war. The Turks were Muslims, and the symbol of Islam is the crescent moon.

She told the students that some people tell the story that in 1529 during the Turkish siege of Vienna, Austria, Viennese bakers heard the noises, alerted the defenders and prevented the fall of the city. In celebration, the bakers formed rolls in the shape of the crescent moon. The rolls became known as **Kipferl** (KIHP-fuhl).

Yvette told the adults to uncover their ears and asked them, "In what country did the **Croissant** originate?" Many of the adults guessed France, and the children joyfully exclaimed, "Wrong! Croissants were first made in Vienna, Austria."

Yvette explained, "My family is from France, where the **Croissant** was made popular. That's why it's eaten by so many people." Many of the children already knew the delicious taste of the crescent-shaped roll.

Yagniza stood slowly, holding a small bag in her hand. She had waited patiently for her turn and felt a bit of sadness and joy as she opened the bag to show her classmates the **Frybread** her mother had made that morning.

She told the class that she was different from most of them because her family and ancestors did not come to the USA by boats or planes. "They have always been here. This has always been their home. But they have not always eaten **Frybread**," she explained.

"**Frybread** was created in the 1800s when Native Americans were forced onto reservations and given rations of flour and lard by the government. From those rations came **Frybread**." Yagniza told the class that Native Americans were the first to cultivate the corn that's used for **Tortillas** and **Cornbread**. When Yagniza passed the **Frybread** around, Chirag said, "In India, we make a bread like this called **Poori** (POOR-ee)."

Hazyl stood in front of the class holding a large loaf of bread that was tan in color. As she broke it in half, she said, "This bread represents who I am: two different colors." One color was a rich dark brown and the other a snowy white. When she first saw the bread she asked her mother, "How can this bread be two colors?" Her mom explained, "Before the bakers put the bread into the oven, they use two different colors of bread dough which are twisted together. When the bread is done, the result is two beautiful colors like you. The lighter part is me and the rich brown color is your dad."

Jason looked on as his heart filled with glee. Then he said, "This bread tells the story of who I am, but my mom is the rich brown color and my dad is the lighter color. The combined colors made me."

The teacher beamed as she looked at all of the breads the children had brought to share with their classmates. She reminded them about what she had said on the day she first told them about this special Show-and-Tell. "Girls and boys come in all sizes, shapes and colors, just like bread. All breads belong to the bread group, and all children belong to the human group, so we are all members of the same family."

"No matter what the color of the bread, it's all good. And no matter what color children are, they are also good," she emphasized.

Next, the children asked Ms. Cherry what breads she ate as a little girl. **"Cornbread** was the bread my family ate, and many of us still do. **Cornbread** was an important part of each meal. We would eat cornbread in the morning for breakfast with milk as a cereal and sometimes with syrup."

The teacher had just one more bread for the children – a **Pretzel** (PRET-suhl). The children felt she had made a big mistake. "**Pretzels** are snacks, not bread!" they exclaimed.

Ms. Cherry explained, "Many people tell the story that **Pretzels** were much larger, and were first baked by monks for breakfast for children with good behavior who said their prayers." **Pretzels** are the only bread made especially for children.

After such a wonderful day, the teacher noted, "There is only one thing left to say. Bread comes in different sizes, shapes, colors, and textures. Even so, it's all bread. Little children come in different sizes, shapes, and colors, but all belong to the same human race, and all children are beautiful."

"So many lessons with so much to learn, " said Ms. Cherry. By now all of the children were wondering when they would taste the breads.

SO THE TEACHER ANNOUNCED "`BON APPETIT!`"

Printed in the United States
By Bookmasters